A Love Affair with Nature

The Story of
Anna Botsford Comstock

Pioneering Naturalist, Artist, Writer, and Teacher

by Cos Ferrara

Acknowledgments

The information in this book comes primarily from two sources.

The first is *The Comstocks of Cornell*, an autobiography written by Anna B. Comstock, as published by in the Cornell Press edition, Ithaca, New York, which is copyright ©1953 by Cornell University. This work benefited from the arrangement of Mrs. Comstock's manuscript by her friend, Glenn W. Herrick, as well as Dr. Francis Wormuth and Dr. Ruby Green Smith.

The handbook lessons in this book, following chapter 7, are:

Reprinted from Anna Botsford Comstock: *Handbook of Nature Study*. Copyright © renewed 1967 by Comstock Publishing Associates, a division of Cornell University Press. Used by permission of the publisher, Cornell University Press. They are lesson numbers 36 and 87.

Anna B. Comstock

A Love Affair with Nature, The Story of Anna Botsford Comstock, Pioneering Naturalist, Artist, Writer, and Teacher, Copyright, © 2004 by Girls Explore™ LLC

All rights reserved. No part of this book may be used or reproduced in any manner whatsoever without written permission of the publisher except in the case of brief quotations embodied in critical articles and reviews. For information address Girls Explore™ LLC, P.O. Box 54, Basking Ridge, NJ 07920, www.girls-explore.com.

Library of Congress Control Number: 2004103770

ISBN 0-9749456-1-7

Printed in the United States of America
10 9 8 7 6 5 4 3 2 1

Photo Permissions:

All photos with the exception of those on pages 104 and 108 are from the following source:

John Henry and Anna Botsford Comstock Papers, 1833-1955, 1874-1932. Collection number 21-23-25. Courtesy of the Division of Rare and Manuscript Collections, Cornell University Library. A list of the photos is below. Please note that many of these photos have been cropped to fit the page, if you look for the photos in the library, please refer to the photo number.

Cover and Pg. 6 – AnnaBotsford 1874	Pg. 50 – The Lodge	Pg. 74 – RMC2004_0394
	Pg. 52 – RMC2004_0387 & RMC2004_0389	Pg. 75 – RMC2004_0400
		Pg. 76 – RMC2004_0386
Pg. 12 – RMC2004_0380	Pg. 55 – RMC2004_0399	Pg. 77 – RMC2004_0407 & RMC2004_0408
Pg. 14 – RMC2004_0381	Pg. 58 – POEM-T ~ 1	
Pg. 21 – RMC2004_0396	Pg. 61 – RMC2004_0398	Pg. 78 – RMC2004_0411
Pg. 25 – RMC2004_0397	Pg. 67 – RMC2004_0409	Pg. 84 – RMC2004_0379
Pg. 27 – Chamberlain Institute	Pg. 68 – RMC2004_0384	Pg. 87 – RMC2004_0393
	Pg. 70 – RMC2004_0402	Pg. 91 – RMC2004_0385
Pg. 30 – RMC2004_0383	Pg. 71 – RMC2004_0403	Pg. 94 – RMC2004_0405
Pg. 37 – RMC2004_0388	Pg. 72 – RMC2004_0401	Pg. 96 – RMC2004_0382
Pg. 49 – RMC2004_0395	Pg. 73 – RMC2004_0406	Pg. 112 – RMC2004_0404

The photos on page 104 and 108 are from Handbook of Nature Study by Anna Botsford Comstock. Copyright © renewed 1967 by Comstock Publishing Associates, a division of Cornell University Press. Used by permission of the publisher, Cornell University Press. Page 104 is from page 359 and page 108 is from page 145.

Cover Design - Chris Kelley – Jon Reis Photo + Design
Interior Design – Vernon Thornblad PoGo Studio

CONTENTS

	Introduction.....................	7
1	Growing Up on a Farm	11
2	Paving the Way at Cornell for Women .	28
3	Who Was John Henry Comstock?.....	39
4	Anna Launches Her Career	48
5	Seeing the World..................	66
6	Driving the Nature Study Movement...	81
7	Anna's *Handbook of Nature Study*	89
	Handbook Lessons for You to Try	100
	List of Anna's Publications	111

Anna B. Comstock

1
Introduction

In the 1890s, farmers in upstate New York were facing a crisis. They couldn't produce enough to support their families. Many of the younger people were leaving the farms. They headed for the cities in search of jobs. Not only were the farm families suffering. Other people throughout New York had to rely more and more on out-of-state farms for their food. This meant they had to pay higher prices.

To deal with this crisis, state officials called together a committee of people concerned about nature. Among these was Anna Botsford Comstock. For years Anna had worked alongside her husband, John, in his scientific study of insects. One phase of their work dealt with the damage that insects can do to plants and crops.

The committee decided to approach the farm problem by educating children in the schools. The thinking was: "If youngsters better understand nature, they will be more successful farmers. Then more of them will stay on the farms and produce."

Though most of the committee members were men, Anna was the ideal person to take a leadership role on this committee. She had grown up on a farm. She had devoted years to examining all forms of nature, many of which can affect farming. She would put specimens under a microscope and illustrate them down to the most minute detail. Her illustrations made it easier for students to learn about nature.

At the time, however, women did not lead committees composed mostly of men. But Anna was used to being the rare female among males. When she entered Cornell University in its first class of women, she was one of 30 females among 800 male students. So Anna was not shaken by being in the minority. And it didn't take long for the other committee members to see that Anna knew much about nature. She also had teaching experience. And she threw herself wholeheartedly into this work. As in other instances, Anna's hard work and intelligence overcame any prejudice against women that committee members may have had.

She visited schools to find out what kinds of programs were in place for teaching nature. There were none. Anna talked to teachers to find out what they knew about nature. Very little. So Anna began to teach groups of teachers about nature study. She wrote and illustrated pamphlets showing teachers how to make nature study fun for students. She set up summer workshops for teachers and taught many of the sessions. And she wrote *Handbook of Nature Study.* This book became "the natural history bible" for generations of teachers.

In plain, everyday language the *Handbook* shows teachers how to make students "investigators," learning about nature by observing it first-hand. The Handbook, first published in 1911, was an immediate success. In fact, it is still reprinted and in use today. The *Handbook* was translated into eight languages, so people in other countries could also benefit from it.

How did this woman assume such a leadership position at a time when such roles were always held by men? She did so by being willing to study hard to get a college education, when few women even finished high school. She taught herself to become an excellent artist of nature's creatures. She became a successful teacher. Anna was never deterred when she heard: "Oh, women just don't do those things." And while she was building a strong professional reputation, Anna was a loving daughter, husband, and friend.

In reading about Anna, you will see what life was like long before people had what we think of today as the common conveniences. You may be surprised at how few opportunities existed for women outside the home. You'll learn how one woman went about quietly but resolutely making a place for women. You'll see how Anna B. Comstock's pioneering spirit helped pave the way for women of the twenty-first century to follow the paths of their own choosing.

1

Growing Up on the Farm

You've probably heard the stories of Abraham Lincoln's early life growing up in a log cabin. Well, Anna Botsford lived at about the same time as Lincoln and she lived in a log cabin. She was born in 1854. She and her family lived on a farm in a rural area of upstate New York. Anna and her neighbors did not have electricity or running water in their homes. Of course, no one traveled by car, communicated by telephone, or were entertained by television or radio. But Anna was a happy child.

The family cabin sat at the edge of an orchard, some distance from the road. Peonies and rosebushes lined the walk to the front door. The family lived in just one large room. At one end was the kitchen and dining area. In the middle was a sitting area with comfortable chairs and rockers. A rag carpet covered the floor. The other end of the room was for sleeping.

Anna slept in a trundle bed. That is a low bed on small wheels. During the day Anna's bed was stored under her parents' bed. At night they rolled it out for Anna. From a window between the beds Anna enjoyed a view of a blooming cinnamon bush. Pretty white curtains bordered the windows. So, while the family was not wealthy, they enjoyed the natural beauty around them. And they added their own touches to make a pleasant home.

Anna's father was a farmer. He was good at doing things with his hands. He also had a good head for business. He was among the first to buy a mower and other machinery. Anna felt her father always seemed to know the right way to do things. And his farm always looked good because of that. The animals were in excellent condition, the fences kept up, and the barns clean.

Anna's father

Mr. Botsford also spent much time reading the

newspaper. Politics and political issues were important to him. He knew the record of every important senator, congressman, and state legislator. Anna's father hated slavery. But he thought the Civil War could have been avoided if the North and South had just talked things out a little more. Anna felt so proud seeing her father up on his horse in his state militia uniform.

She enjoyed his clever wit and keen sense of humor. She admired him for being kindhearted and generous to the unfortunate. On many occasions, the Botsfords played host to people who had some serious troubles. Anna's parents provided comfort in the form of food, clothing, and spiritual encouragement. Once a group of traveling Indians stopped at Anna's home to barter some goods. When a severe rainstorm hit, Anna's mother and father invited the Indians to stay in their home for the night and until the storm stopped.

Much of Anna's love of nature, sense of humor, dedication to work, and commitment to the world can be traced to her father.

Anna also took much from her mother. Mrs. Botsford had a passionate love for the beauty of nature. She often took Anna for walks in the woods and fields. She taught Anna the names of the many flowers as well as the constellations in the night sky. She once told Anna that "Heaven may be a happier place than the earth, but it cannot be more beautiful." From her mother, Anna came to appreciate the natural wonders. She carried that love

Anna's mother

throughout her life and built her career on it.

She also took from her mother a love of reading, especially stories and poetry. Anna recalled her mother's putting her to sleep at night not by singing lullabies but by reciting poetry. From these moments, Anna gained a love of rhythm and rhyme.

Mrs. Botsford had what Anna called "a sunny disposition." She believed that everyone meant to do right, even if it didn't seem that way. She refused to listen to critical gossip. She enjoyed work and was an excellent seamstress. She could "spin flax and weave woolen cloth and linen of beautiful, intricate patterns." She was a good cook and always kept her house neat and "homey."

In those days, people living in rural areas and on farms could not easily get to a doctor. Nor could a doctor get to them. So people had to take care of one another. Mrs. Botsford spent many a night nursing a sick neighbor back to health. Anna saw her mother as being strong of body, cheerful in spirit, courageous, capable, peace loving, and self-sacrificing. Anna grew up to be much like her mother in all of these ways.

Growing Up on the Farm

For the most part, the family was self-supporting. That is, most of what they ate came from their farm and their own hands. They raised wheat and corn, which were ground in the village mill into their own breadstuff. They raised their own vegetables, potatoes, and apples. They spun yarn from their own sheep. They made enough maple sugar to carry the family for a year. They killed their own meat and cured hams.

The family earned money to buy items such as tea, coffee, spices, cotton cloth, needles, thread, and shoes. One source of this money was Mrs. Botsford's cheeses. She made great cheeses and sold them. Mr. Botsford also earned money by "breaking" steers. He was skillful at training oxen, and farmers paid him well for this service.

Anna's father and mother had both been married to other spouses before they married each other. In each case the spouse died. There were no children from those marriages, but Anna's mother and father stayed in touch with their deceased spouses' families. So Anna had four—not two—sets of "grandparents" loving her, as well as numerous "aunts" and "uncles."

When Anna was three years old, the family left the log cabin and moved to a house at the edge of the forest. They still had the farm. This house was larger, with more rooms. With a large cheesehouse right on the property, Mrs. Botsford made dozens of cheeses and stored them there. Cheeses weighing 30 to 40 pounds each would be lined up on rows of benches. Between the cheesehouse and the barn sat the water pump. (Remember, these people could not enjoy the convenience of indoor plumbing.) Across the road were a horse barn and a cow barn. These were "fascinating places in which to play," Anna recalled.

Though the Botsfords lived on a farm, they had many pleasant neighbors not too far away. These people had good intelligence and eager minds. During summer, families spent evenings visiting one another. In winter, they attended dances, often in the empty cheesehouses. Anna beamed as she watched her father dance gracefully across the floor.

Peddlers also broke up the routine of daily living. These men moved from village to village, farm to farm selling various kinds of goods. Anna recalled one of her favorites—"The Old Scotchman." He sold linens. He dressed in Scottish-style clothes and wore a tam-o'shanter. That is a soft, round, woolen cap, often with a tassel in the center. He loved children and carried a bagful of candies for them. Another favorite was the tin peddler. He drove a horse and wagon. This handsome man told great stories and sang songs. These peddlers were always welcome and usually were invited to stay for dinner.

Anna had friends her own age to play with. A favorite was a neighbor, boy named Herbert Norbert. She remembered him as quiet (while Anna was talkative.) He, like Anna, was an only child. Both had learned to read at an early age. Herbert and Anna spent much time together reading, and then discussing with each other what they had read. Anna wrote about her feelings for Herbert: "No girl could have been more fortunate than I in an intimate boy companionship."

After Herbert and his family moved away, Anna spent a lot of time with her four cousins—all boys. They were bright, happy, well-behaved boys.

Anna attended a small rural schoolhouse about a half-mile from home. All students, regardless of age or grade, shared the same room. One teacher taught all of the children. For a three-month session in winter, a man taught the classes. That was because the bigger boys attended school in winter. The rest of the year the big boys were needed to work on the farms. The only children in school for those sessions were girls and younger boys. For these sessions, a woman taught.

Very often the teacher did not live in the area. She would come for the few months and then return to her home. For the time she was assigned as teacher, she would board with families of the students. She would spend about a week with one family, then move on to another, and so on.

Anna enjoyed the time when the teachers boarded at her home. They always seemed to bring new ideas to the dinner conversation. Anna recalled that one teacher read to the family from an astronomy book. Anna and her parents sat silent and fascinated by this "new information" about the stars.

Getting to and from school in winter could be hard. Sometimes the road was so buried by snow that the men would drive their teams of oxen to cut a path for the children to follow. Anna recalled a heroic teacher who led the smaller children home in a snowstorm. He held his shawl in front of the children to shield their eyes from the blinding snow. By the time the teacher had gotten the last of the children home, his hands were frostbitten.

The Civil War began in 1861, when Anna was seven years old. It ended in 1865, when she was 11. The war made a strong impression on Anna. She had a number of cousins in the army. When they came home on leave, they'd visit the farm. Anna admired how handsome they looked in their uniforms. She'd sit spellbound, taking in their first-hand accounts of the battlefield horrors. She also read accounts of battles in the newspaper. Studying the maps to see where the different battles were fought taught her much about the geography of the United States.

Anna did her part in the war effort. She scraped linen with a knife to make lint for bandages. Nurses used these to dress the soldiers' wounds. She also helped knit stockings and wristlets for the soldiers. When they heard that President Lincoln had died from an assassin's bullet, Anna and her family felt a terrible sadness come over their home.

Like most children growing up on a farm, Anna began working at an early age. Before she was four years old, Anna had learned to sew. By age six, she could knit. From the time she was seven, if she wanted new woolen stockings, she knit them herself. Before she was 10, Anna had pieced together a bedquilt. She took small pieces of cloth from many different places (and people) and sewed one to the other. She saw each piece in her quilt as a memento of a garment she (or a friend) had worn years earlier.

Anna also had chores to perform around the house. Before leaving for school in the morning, she washed the breakfast dishes. (Remember, there were no dishwashers then.) She also had to wash out the milk pails. Milk was not delivered or purchased in bottles or cartons but taken in pails from the cows. Then she swept up the dining area and kitchen. In the evening, she washed the supper dishes and the milk pails again. Then she'd go into the garden to dig up potatoes for the next day's meal. She fed the chickens and cared for her canary.

Anna's mother had good taste in clothes and kept pace with the fashions of the times. She saw to it that Anna always had a "best dress" for special occasions.

One of Anna's joys in summer was going barefoot. And her favorite game was pretending to be a princess. She'd prance around the house or the yard elegantly, her nose in the air, her arm raised. She played that game until her mother told her princesses always wore shoes and stockings. Anna never played the game again. That's how much she liked being barefoot.

In the rural area where Anna lived, people made their own entertainment most of the time. But once a year, everyone got excited because the traveling circus came to town, not far from where Anna lived. Anna loved it all, especially the beautiful circus ladies in their spangled costumes riding atop their elegant horses. These ladies put their horses through a series of tricks that wowed the audience. They'd also stand atop the horses as they trotted around the rink. At home, Anna would dress up and mount the family's old mare, pretending to do the tricks she had seen at the circus.

Another special event was the agricultural fair. Farmers from miles around got together to display their prize animals and crops. Women exhibited their home-baked goods and crafts. In the "ladies pavilion," Anna was enthralled by the beautiful flowers, plants, pictures, quilts, embroidered linen, wreaths, beaded skirts, cushions, and mats. Besides all the new things to see, the fair meant Anna and her family had an opportunity to stop work and spend time with friends.

When Anna was 10 years old, the family moved again. This was Anna's third home and the first in which she had her own room. It was small and plain but had a beautiful view of the orchard.

Another good feature of the new house was that it was just across the road from the schoolhouse. Anna recalled that, for the first time, she was "naughty" in school. Until then, Anna had always been a good student and mindful of her teachers. But the teacher she had that year was, in Anna's words, "unfitted for teaching." One day the teacher was about to whip Anna. In those days teachers often used a whip to discipline unruly children. This teacher took

Growing Up on the Farm

Anna's home

down the long appletree switch, but before she could touch Anna, Anna ran out of the school into a cornfield. The teacher came after her, but the young girl crept quietly among the corn stalks. The teacher couldn't find her. After about 30 minutes, while the other children in the school were going wild, the teacher gave up looking for Anna. The next day, Anna returned to school and took her seat as if nothing had happened.

But the battle of wills between Anna and this teacher was not over. The teacher was instructing the children in the rules of English grammar. Anna asked for the reasons behind these rules, so she could better understand them. This annoyed the teacher, so she said: "Anna does not seem to get along as well as the rest of the class; hereafter

I will hear her recite by herself." The teacher thought she'd embarrass Anna into behaving. Anna asked: "Will you hear me recite all I can learn?" "Of course," the teacher answered. So Anna took up her grammar book and began to study it. She had always had a good memory and mastered most of the book. The next afternoon, the teacher called upon Anna to recite. Anna stood and started reciting. She gave one rule after another. A few times the teacher tried to stop Anna, but defiant Anna said: "You promised to hear all I could learn."

Perhaps these incidents and this teacher were planted firmly in Anna's mind. Years later, when she became a teacher, she treated her students very differently. And she remembered those days when she was giving teachers instructions on how to teach.

Anna's "naughtiness" may have been stirred partly by her dislike for that teacher. It may also have been her age. At about the same time, she and a schoolmate—a sweet, refined girl—began swearing. When the two of them were alone, they used every foul word and phrase they had ever heard. One day they saw a caterpillar on a fence and began swearing at it. The caterpillar lifted the front part of its body and swung back and forth. The girls took that as a sign that they shouldn't be swearing. That was the last time they did.

When Anna was 13, the family moved again. Her new home would be farther away from the school but closer to the village called Otto. Anna enjoyed the thrill of more new adventures, new friends, and a new house. Here's how she later described her new home:

> The house was on a hillside above the road, with an orchard at one side and behind it, and it made a pretty picture. The view from the piazza (porch) was eastward across a wide valley, with a stream winding in and out of the "kneeling hills." It was from this piazza that I learned to observe the exquisite pale coloring of the eastern sky at sunset.

Even as a young child, Anna had a good eye for detail. This talent no doubt helped her in later years when she did illustrations for books and magazines.

Anna attended the school in Otto. This school was much larger than the one she had gone too earlier. In this school Anna saw older students taking lessons in oil painting. She wanted to join them. At first, however, she would have to settle for drawing lessons.

She was very impressed by the teachers in this school in Otto. They were bright and knowledgeable. They treated students firmly but fairly. Two of them became her lifelong friends.

One of the many friends Anna made at this school was a girl named Etta Holbrook. Etta lived with an aunt and uncle—Mr. and Mrs. Allen—in Otto. Mrs. Allen had been a teacher and Mr. Allen was one of the wealthiest men in the area. They had a beautiful home. On stormy nights, when Anna could not make the one-mile journey home, she stayed with Etta at the Allens' home. Mrs. Ann French Allen was the person who aroused Anna's ambition to attend college. Watching and listening to Mrs. Allen, Anna one day decided: "I want the work I do in this world to be the best I can do and to make it count."

The school in Otto was more than a one-room schoolhouse. It had rooms enough to separate the younger children from the older. When Anna was 14, the teacher of the primary children became sick. Anna was asked to take over that class for the final six weeks of the term. It was difficult but Anna loved it.

She also liked the money she earned—three dollars a week. At the end of the term she had saved $18. Anna told her father she wanted to use her money to buy books. He said: "Let's make a family holiday out of it." So the family journeyed to Fredonia, New York. Anna found a bookstore and bought her books. Many of them were books Mrs. Allen had recommended to her. They included books by Shakespeare and Dickens. She also bought collections of poetry by some of the greatest poets in the English language. These books were still standing on Anna's bookshelves in her home on the day she died in 1930.

Her choice of books is interesting. Though she had a love of nature and made her career studying it, she also loved the arts. Her varied interests and backgrounds had much to do with her overall success later as artist, writer, naturalist, speaker, and teacher.

When Anna was ready for high school, there was none in Otto. She had to attend a private school, Chamberlain Institute, in a town called Randolph, 18

Anna at 18

miles away from home. Anna recalled that the teachers—all men—were bright and talented. The other students, boys and girls, were "brilliant." One of the students she met there, Martha Van Rensselaer, would later join Anna on the faculty at Cornell.

The Chamberlain Institute offered after-school activities and Anna took advantage of many of them. As a member of the literary society she debated and gave speeches. She won prizes for her oratory (speeches). She worked on the newspaper staff. Overall, Anna loved Chamberlain. She learned a great deal and had fun with the girls and boys.

One unpleasant experience at Chamberlain was the pressure on her to "experience religion." Anna knew her own mind. She resented the attempts students and faculty at Chamberlain made to influence her into thinking the way they did, to hold their beliefs.

In 1873, Anna graduated from Chamberlain. One of the top students in her class, she was asked to give the salutatory address. That is the welcome given at graduation ceremony. Anna gave her entire speech in Latin.

Anna later recalled that at Chamberlain she had learned to study. She met cultivated people. She made many happy friendships. She had "boy friends," too, but none too serious. It was quite common at the time for girls to wed soon after graduating from high school, but that was not Anna's plan. Her eyes were fixed on a college education and couldn't let anything—including a boy—interfere with that.

Growing Up on the Farm

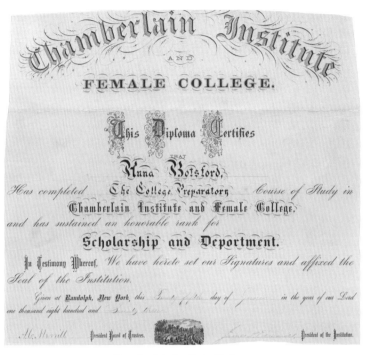

Chamberlain Institute Diploma

2
Paving the Way at Cornell for Women

$\mathbf{I}$n the early 1870s, very few colleges or universities accepted women students. So it was with great excitement that Mrs. Allen showed Anna a newspaper clipping announcing that the university in Ann Arbor, Michigan, was enrolling its first female students. But Michigan was a long distance away from Otto, New York. "Too far away," Anna thought. But there was another possibility she would soon learn about.

While Anna was in her last year at Chamberlain Institute, a recent graduate of the school stopped by one day. He attended Cornell University, which is in upstate New York. He said Cornell planned to enroll its first class of women. He suggested that Anna think about applying for admission to Cornell. He said: "It is a great place for an education; but if you go there, you won't have such a gay time as you have had here (at Chamberlain), for the boys there won't pay any attention to the college girls."

Anna thought about what he had said and then concluded: "Cornell must be a good place for a girl to get an education; it has all the advantages of a university and a convent combined." Anna, who always enjoyed a good time, wasn't going to college for the social life. If she somehow managed to go to college, it would be to get an education.

Anna started at Cornell in 1874. But to be fully admitted to the freshman class, she would first have to pass some exams. One of these tested her knowledge of the German language. Though Anna had studied some German, she didn't know it well enough to get her through an exam.

She found out who the professor in charge of these exams was. It was a Bela P. Mackoon. From the men at Cornell, Anna found out that Professor Mackoon struck terror into the hearts of his students. "But he is an excellent teacher," they said. Before approaching this frightening man who would determine whether or not she could stay at Cornell, Anna went to take a look at him. She noticed that he wore a Masonic pin on his lapel. That meant he was a member of the Masonic Order, a fraternal group with

Anna and her friends in a room at Sage Hall

chapters throughout the United States. Anna recognized the pin because her father was a member of the same organization. Before she left home for school, her father had given her his Masonic pin and a letter from his lodge. "Anna," he said, "if you ever find yourself in a crisis, and need help right away, you can always turn to one of my Masonic 'brothers.'" Obediently, Anna took the pin and the letter from her father. She never thought she would use them.

She made an appointment to see Professor Mackoon. When she entered his office, she presented her credentials—including her father's Masonic pin and letter. "He could not have been kinder to me," she recalled. The professor arranged for Anna to come to him for the lessons she needed to pass the German exam. And she would not have to pay anything for these lessons. Anna took the lessons and passed the exam. She then took her place among the first group of women students at Cornell University.

Just think. Anna was one of about 30 young women attending school with hundreds of men. It must have been a challenge. These men were not used to seeing women as "scholars." Of course, they knew women in social settings, but many could think of women only in those terms. They could not envision women on an equal footing with them in the classrooms and laboratories at the university. Anna and her "sisters" would eventually change that thinking. But it wouldn't be easy and it would take time. Anna did not shy away from the challenge.

There was no dormitory for the women students yet. So Anna boarded at a private home, where a few other students also had rooms. The students—men and women—ate meals together in the house dining room. Several male students from Brazil were among those taking meals with Anna.

One day early in her first term at Cornell, Anna was feeling blue and homesick. Having to take two more unexpected entrance exams also upset her. To make matters worse, when she got back to the house, she found a letter from home. The woman of the house had placed it on Anna's plate in the dining room. Instead of cheering her up, this letter had the opposite effect. Anna felt more homesick than ever. She could feel the tears forming. She didn't want the others to see her lose her self-control, she ran into the next room.

After a few minutes she composed herself and returned to the dining room. To her surprise, she found the Brazilian men weeping. They felt the pangs of homesickness, too. Anna took heart from their sympathetic response and began to smile. Seeing her smile, the men smiled too. Then they all began to laugh. They all ate their dinner in good cheer.

Despite being from different cultures, Anna and these Brazilian students became good friends. Learning about people different from yourself is one of the major benefits of attending college. But Anna found that some people hold on to prejudices. A few weeks after the dining room tear-and-laughter incident, one of the Brazilian men invited Anna to attend the Thanksgiving Day ball with him. Anna said she would be delighted. She wrote a letter home asking her mother to ship Anna's two formal dresses to her.

Not knowing much about social customs at Cornell, Anna sought some advice. She called on the Vice President of the university—Professor Russell—and told him of the situation. He advised Anna not to attend the ball with the Brazilian man. "He's a foreigner," Professor Russell said. "Their customs are different from ours."

"But I've already promised him I'd go with him," Anna said.

Though they disagreed, Anna and Professor Russell had a pleasant conversation. They would become friends for many years. On this occasion, Anna thanked him for his advice. But she went to the ball with her Brazilian friend. "No Puritan youth could have treated me with more courtesy and respect," she recalled. "I enjoyed it all greatly." Later she added: "Professor Russell was certainly wrong about the Brazilian students whom I knew. They were all gentlemen, by our standards as well as their own."

The young Brazilian man was not the only male student to show an interest in Anna. Despite what her friend from Chamberlain had told her, the men at Cornell did pay attention to the "college girls." The woman in whose house Anna was living moved some furniture around to create a sitting room on the first floor so Anna and other women could have a place to sit and talk with their many male visitors.

After her initial bout of homesickness, Anna found her days at Cornell busy and happy. When spring came, she and her friends took long walks in the woods for botany class. They'd go boating on Cayuga Lake. Two other men who lived in the same house, who were excellent students, became Anna's good companions. One of these—Will Berry—became a special friend. For a short time the two were engaged to be married. But as Anna wrote later: "The affair fell by its own weight. It was too emotional to meet the realities of life."

The following year, all of the women students lived together in Sage Hall. The sophomores waged friendly battles against the freshmen, and everyone enjoyed them.

One night the women students got together for a serious talk. This was now their second year at Cornell and they decided the time had come to set some guidelines for their behavior. One was to abolish the practice of bowing to the men as they passed on campus. Somehow, when the women first arrived on campus, they showed respect for the men already there by bowing. The women thought this practice was degrading. So they decided as a group to stop doing it. At first the men were a little surprised, but they soon got over it.

The women also asserted themselves in another way. The President of the university thought the women should have a chaperone in charge of Sage Hall. But the students considered that "insulting to our integrity." They made a strong case before the president and they won. There would be no chaperone watching over them.

These actions make it clear that Anna and her friends would not be intimidated. Though women in college was a new concept, and they were far outnumbered, these women stood their ground. They would not let anyone treat them as second-class citizens. In this and in many other ways, Anna and her sisters paved the way for others. They were making it easier for future generations of women students to get an education as equals.

Anna enjoyed a happy social life at Sage Hall. The building was close to the gymnasium, so it was easy to get to the dances held there every Friday night. She and her sister students also enjoyed musicals and readings of Shakespeare and modern writers.

Many of the other women students in Sage Hall were interesting personalities with a great deal of talent. One,

Julia Thomas, later became president of Wellesley College, a top-notch women's college in Massachusetts. Martha Carey Thomas became President of Bryn Mawr College, an equally respected women's school in Pennsylvania. Harriet May Mills became a leader in the fight for women's suffrage—the right to vote.

Anna found the course work challenging. But she also felt it gave her a new sense of life. She especially enjoyed History of the Reformation. This religious movement took place in Europe in the 1500s. The professor for the course, Dr. White, was also president of the university. Anna loved the way he interwove the history with literature, art, architecture, and music. Anna spent many hours in the library reading additional materials about the subject. In all, she read 30 books in one term. "My mind and my vision expanded in leaps," she later wrote.

In another course, on German literature, Anna had a different kind of experience. Part of the course centered around German folk tales. As a young girl, Anna had read many of these same tales from a children's book a neighbor had given her. In discussing the tales in the course, the teacher was impressed with Anna's knowledge of German folklore. He complimented her. "I think you must have given much time to it," he said.

"Yes, I have given many happy hours to it," she answered. She didn't bother explaining that those hours had been spent many years before when Anna was a young girl.

Among the many social events at Cornell were the Delta Upsilon Quarterlies. These were delightful informal dances. Anna recalled especially a mask and costume dance. Anna took great pains in creating her costume. Her description of it shows her imagination and creativity, as well as her ability to form vivid word pictures:

> Personifying "night," I wore a long drapery of black tarlatan (thin, stiff muslin like the material in a ballerina's skirt). It was set with silver stars, and a black silk gown that trailed. My long black hair was loose, the tarlatan veil was fastened on my forehead with a silver ornament, and my black domino (mask) was edged with stars. I was a somber figure, but no one had more fun at that dance than I.

In the winter of 1875, Anna enrolled in a zoology class (the study of animal life). This experience would have a great impact on her life. A young man named John Henry Comstock taught the class. He was a Cornell student at the time who also lectured in zoology. Anna showed a great interest in the course work, and that may have been why Mr. Comstock showed such an interest in Anna. Maybe not. Whatever the reason, he spent much time with her after class showing her the thousands of insects he had collected in his small laboratory.

He also came to call on her many times at Sage Hall. But the relationship was purely one of friendship, because he had a "special relationship" with another woman, Jennie Bartlett. Jennie was a victim of tuberculosis, an infectious disease affecting many parts of the body, especially the lungs. She and her mother had gone to Florida in hopes of overcoming the illness. Before leaving, Jennie suggested that Anna and Mr. Comstock spend time with one another. (At that time, it was proper for a young woman to refer to a young male friend as "Mister," until they got to know each other very well.)

In the fall of that year, Mr. Comstock took his meals at Sage Hall. He secretly arranged with the landlady to be seated next to Anna. They enjoyed each other's company, and with others at the table, had many a good laugh. Anna and Mr. Comstock would go for walks in the woods and occasionally take a drive in a horse drawn wagon. Still their relationship was one only of friendship. "We understand each other," Anna wrote, "which is why we are so thoroughly friends."

In the following spring, Mr. Comstock went to Florida to be closer to the ailing Jennie. While there, he explored the countryside. He was amazed at the different kinds of insect

John as a young man

specimens he found in that part of the United States. As her health continued to fail, Jennie decided that she could not marry Mr. Comstock. She released him from any sense of obligation he may have had to her. When he returned to Cornell, only Anna knew how upset he was. Rumors began to fly about him and Anna. She said those rumors "amused us because they were so unfounded."

In time, however, that would change.

3

Who Was John Henry Comstock?

John Henry Comstock did not enjoy the warm, pleasant childhood that Anna did. His early years were much like those of a child in a Charles Dickens novel. He was born in Wisconsin, in February, 1849. That year, prospectors discovered gold in California. Like thousands of others, the boy's father felt the urge to go west in search of a fortune. So he kissed his wife, Susan, and his son—whom they called Henry—and off he went.

Mrs. Comstock was left to care for her son alone. Her husband had hired a man to tend to the farm until he returned. But Mr. Comstock didn't return. He contracted cholera (a disease of the stomach and intestines). He died on the way to California. Adding to that tragedy, the man left in charge of the farm was a swindler. Soon Mrs. Comstock didn't have money enough to pay the mortgage on the farm. The farm was taken from her. She had to sell off all of her possessions to pay her debts. She and Henry then began a series of stays with various relatives in different parts of the country.

Eventually the two made their way to upstate New York, where Mrs. Comstock had family. She took a job as a housekeeper for a family to earn money to live on. But she became very ill and had to give up her work. She could not care for Henry or support him. The boy was put in an orphanage—a group home for children without parents.

He endured the terrible conditions there for some time before his mother's uncle came to visit him. Uncle Daniel became so upset seeing the conditions in which Henry was living, he took the boy to live with him. This arrangement was to last only until Henry's mother was well enough to care for him herself. Uncle Daniel brought the boy to live with him in his mountain home. Henry was now five years old.

While Mrs. Comstock was recovering, she thought she could learn to be a nurse. This would be a good way to earn money for herself and Henry. In time she took a job as a private nurse in a home in Schenectady, New York, some miles away. Henry left Uncle Daniel and the mountain home. But as things turned out, the boy could not live with his mother in the home where she worked and lived.

So he was sent to live with other relatives—Aunt Alma and Uncle John.

Henry loved Aunt Alma, who was very gentle. But Uncle John handed out stern discipline, often with a whip. One of Henry's chores was to wash the dishes. Every time he dropped and broke one, he'd get a whipping. Henry stuttered as a youngster and Uncle John thought the way to correct that was with the whip. Every time the boy stuttered or stammered, he'd get another whipping. In letters to his mother, Henry would tell her how much he missed her. But he never complained of the treatment he was receiving.

Fortunately for Henry, Uncle John received an offer of a position in another town. He had to move and could not take the boy with him. He left Henry with neighbors, the Green family.

Henry lived with the Green family on their farm for some time. When he was 11, he had earned enough money to make a trip by train to Schenectady, where his mother was living. As luck would have it, a rainstorm washed out the bridge, and the train could not continue. Henry had to make his way back to the Greens' farm.

But on his way, he stopped at a farmhouse for a drink. The family there treated him with kindness and warmth. The Turners asked where he was traveling to and from. He wound up telling them just about his whole life story.

They felt sorry for the boy and offered to have him live with them. "We'll try it for a few months," Mr. Turner said. "If it's not right for you, you'll tell us and you can go on your way. If it's not right for us, we'll tell you and you'll be on your way. We'll clothe and feed you. In return, you'll have to do whatever we ask of you. You can go to school three months in winter, but you'll have to help with farm chores the rest of the year." Henry agreed to those terms.

Mr. Turner was a retired sea captain turned farmer. He was a kind man. Henry called him "Pa Lewis." He called Mrs. Turner "Ma Becky." They both came to love Henry as one of their own sons.

There were three Turner sons, and all three were seamen. Because the brothers were away at sea most of the time, Henry received much attention from Pa Lewis and Ma Becky. Working alongside Pa Lewis in the fields, Henry became close to nature. He especially loved the many insects that populated the farm. That spurred his interest in insects that would grow throughout his life.

When the Turner brothers returned home from the sea, Henry enjoyed playing games with them. Each time they were ready to ship out again, he wanted to join them. When he became old enough, Ma Becky felt he wasn't strong enough. "You're too frail," Ma Becky said. "Sailing requires a strong back, which you don't have." But she knew how much he wanted to go, so she came up with an idea. "Every ship needs a good steward," she said, "and you can certainly learn to cook."

So Henry learned to cook, and soon he was at sea

with his "brothers." Once there, he did more than cook. He also learned about sailing. And he spent a good deal of time reading whatever books he could get his hands on.

When he was home again for the winter and attending school, his teacher, Miss Eleanor Dickinson, said: "Henry, you're far ahead of the other students. You should be learning from more advanced textbooks." Henry walked five miles to buy an Algebra book. Miss Dickinson worked with him at the end of the day after the other children left to help him learn Algebra. That book and those lessons opened a new world to him. So did Miss Dickinson. She was the person who most influenced his desire to get an education.

To raise the money to continue his education in high school, Henry went to sea again. But unfortunately he got sick and had to go home. The rule was: "No work. No money." But he applied for admission to Mexico Academy in New York state and managed to get a job sweeping floors at the school to pay his tuition.

He studied the classics—Greek and Latin—as well as science, art, music, grammar, and math. He also learned a number of foreign languages, which helped him later with his science work. He loved the school and did well there. He did so well he began thinking of career choices. Most people suggested he think about becoming a doctor, a lawyer, or a minister. But in the back of his mind Henry thought of becoming a scientist—one who studies various forms of nature.

On one sea excursion, the ship made a stop in Buffalo. Going ashore, Henry shopped the bookstores. In one he asked the clerk if the store kept any books on non-flowering plants. "I don't know," the clerk said, shrugging his shoulders. "All the science books are over there. Search for yourself."

Henry browsed through the shelves and skimmed through each book. He came across Insects Injurious to Vegetation, by Thaddeus W. Harris. The book fascinated him. He read about how insects can do damage to plants and endanger people's food supply. He also loved the many illustrations in the book that made ideas so much clearer than the words alone.

He wanted to buy the book but the price was ten dollars. Henry didn't have that much. So he ran back to the ship and asked the captain if he could have an advance on his salary. He got it, returned to the store, and bought the book. Whenever he had spare time, he buried his nose in that book. Even as he washed dishes in the ship's galley, he stood the book in front of him and learned about the order of insects. By the end of that sea journey, Henry knew what he wanted to do in his life. "But," he asked himself, "can I make a living studying insects?"

In 1869, Henry entered Cornell University. He chose Cornell for a number of reasons. First it was not too far from the Turners' farm. Second, the school planned to teach many courses in science, Henry's main interest. And third, students could do jobs around campus that would help them earn money for tuition. Henry had always had to pay or work his own way through school and the world. He was glad to get the chance to do it again.

After just five weeks at Cornell, Henry came down with malaria and had to go home. When he recovered, he had missed too much of the term to return. So he'd have to wait for the winter term. While waiting, Henry taught at the local school. This was the start of a teaching career that lasted a lifetime.

The next term, Henry returned to Cornell. He proved to be a very hard-working and intelligent student. Professor Wilder, the head of the Zoology Department, asked Henry to be his assistant. "Great," Henry thought. He would be working with a man he admired in a field he loved. And he would be receiving money for his work that could go toward paying his tuition.

While taking courses and working in the zoology lab, Henry also studied entomology (the study of insects) on his own. At the time there was no professor of entomology at the school, but one was scheduled to arrive the following year. Just before the term started, Dr. Wilder discovered the professor would not be coming to Cornell. Rather than cancel the course, he asked Henry to teach it. Imagine. While still a student himself, Henry would also be teaching a course to his fellow students.

Henry had very little to work with in teaching entomology. The school had only a few books on the subject and no money to buy others. The books they did have had been given as gifts. Henry began setting up a laboratory, but he didn't even have a microscope. Despite the lack of equipment, he was determined to give his students as much knowledge of entomology as possible.

He began by collecting specimens of insects and cataloging them. He wouldn't just tell his students about the insects. He would show them. And he would have the students go into the woods and find specimens themselves. He would then show them how to observe the insects they had found and record their observations. The course was a huge success.

When Henry received his bachelor's degree in June 1874, many friends suggested he study to become a doctor. In a letter to Ma Becky he wrote: "I prefer being a naturalist."

Dr. Wilder was pleased with Henry's choice and offered him a position teaching entomology (the study of insects) at Cornell. And there he stayed for the rest of his life. He never went on for an advanced degree, as most university professors do. But Henry learned so much by reading and observation. He undertook assignments for the United States Department of Agriculture to study the impact of various insects on farming in different parts of the country. He always looked beyond the scientific aspect to see how farmers and their families and people as a whole were affected by what he found in nature.

He was invited to give talks and conduct seminars in many states. He wrote textbooks and articles on the subject. In his classes he often had students with advanced degrees. But even these admired Henry's knowledge and ability to teach it.

Of all the students who attended Henry's classes, one would hold a special place. That student would become his partner for life. That student was Anna Botsford.

4
Anna Launches Her Career

Good friends since the day they met, Anna and Henry had much in common. Uppermost was their love for nature. That common interest solidified their affection for one another. Over the Christmas vacation, Henry went with Anna to spend some time with her family.

It soon became clear to Anna's parents that this friendship might blossom into romance. Mr. Botsford liked Henry's willingness to work hard. He saw that, if Anna and Henry were to marry, Henry would provide for his daughter. Mrs. Botsford liked Henry's manner, especially in the way he treated Anna. For some reason, though, they referred to Henry as "Harry." Anna, too, began calling him Harry, and did throughout their life together. So from this point on in Anna's story, John Henry Comstock is referred to as "Harry."

In October 1878, Anna and Harry were married. Ironically, on the same day, Anna's childhood friend, Herbert Northrup, was to be married. Not wanting to disappoint a friend, Anna and Harry attended Herbert's

Anna and John's wedding certificate

wedding in the morning and returned to Otto for their own wedding in the afternoon. Anna obviously was not a typical bride, or a typical friend.

The couple's first home was on the Cornell campus—a little house they called Fall Creek Cottage. Though the house was small, Anna and Harry received guests their frequently, including family and friends, colleagues from the college, and students.

Comstock home at Cornell

From the start, Anna took part in Harry's work. She organized his laboratory. She wrote his business letters. At one point, Harry said: "If I can have diagrams and illustrations of my specimens, I could make my lectures so much more meaningful to the students." Anna happily took on the challenge. At first she worked with basic instruments—India ink, pens, a drafting board, and a

T-square. She would examine an insect under a microscope and then sketch what she saw. Her drawings worked so well because they were not only clear but also accurate. As she performed these different tasks, Anna was developing her artistic skill. She was also learning more and more about insects and nature.

At the same time that Anna was working, she had a house to run. In the 19th century when Anna lived, it was not common for a wife to work outside the home. Most wives were expected to tend to the house and family. Today, that has changed somewhat. Many wives work outside the home. While husbands often share the housework and child-rearing with their wives, in many cases the woman still carries the heavier portion of the house-and-family burden.

In a letter to her mother, Anna explained that being organized enabled her to balance her housework and her professional work:

- Monday: forenoon (morning) do the washing; afternoon, laboratory
- Tuesday: laboratory
- Wednesday: forenoon, iron; afternoon, odds and ends of housework
- Thursday: cook and bake, afterwards laboratory
- Friday: laboratory
- Saturday: sweep and dust the house from top to bottom and mop the kitchen

Anna as a young woman   *John Henry Comstock*

Not long after they were married, Harry received a grant to investigate the cotton worm in the southern part of the United States. Anna helped Harry write the report he filed on his findings. On the strength of that report, Harry was given a position with the Department of Agriculture in Washington D. C. He took a leave of absence from Cornell for two years. He and Anna went to live and work in the nation's capital.

Anna frequently went to the office with Harry and worked there. She wrote letters and took entomological notes. As farmers and agricultural magazines sent questions to the Department of Agriculture, Anna answered them. One day the Department's Commissioner came into the office and saw all that Anna was doing.

"How much are you paid?" he asked.

"Nothing," Anna replied. "I do it because I like the work and I help my husband help the farmers of the country."

The Commissioner was shocked. "For all you do," he said, "you should be paid." He saw to it that Anna was added to the payroll and would receive a regular salary.

Anna loved doing the work. Receiving a salary for her work added to her sense of accomplishment. She began to realize that she, too, could be self-sufficient. That was a novel idea for women in the 19th century. It was through the pioneering efforts of women like Anna that self-sufficient women became accepted.

Recognizing the number of letters that Anna sent out daily, and the lengthy reports she worked up, Harry brought a modern innovation into the office—a typewriter.

An issue that concerned Harry very much was the devastation that scale bugs were causing on citrus fruit in Florida and California. (Scale bugs are small insects whose bodies are covered with a waxy film. Their mouths can pierce and suck. *Aphids* and *cicadas* are two kinds of scale bugs.)

While Harry went to Florida to observe the scale bugs and collect specimens, Anna stayed in Washington to run the office. Aside from handling the normal day-today business, she cataloged the specimens as Harry sent them in. When someone asked her if she felt lonely with her husband away, Anna replied: "I find life too full for loneliness."

By the time Harry returned to Washington, the report on the cotton worm in the South had been given to members of Congress. They praised the work done and allotted more money for Harry to go to California to investigate the scale bug there. Anna went with him. While he was doing the field work, Anna took charge of the lab they were using for the project.

In addition to their work, they made a side trip for personal reasons. Some years before, Harry's mother had moved from New York to California, to work with the family that had hired her. While there, she met a gentleman and eventually married him. So Harry and Anna took the opportunity to visit his mother while they were in California. That was the first time Harry had seen his mother since he was 13 years old.

Harry could not possibly preserve all of the specimens he was finding. So Anna busily sketched many of them. In some of the drawings Anna captured different habits these little creatures engaged in. That information went a long way in explaining the insect's behavior and its effect on plants.

Harry was intent on completing his research on the scale bugs and publishing it. Anna gave three days of every week to studying these creatures under a microscope and then drawing them. Here's how she did it:

> With an eyepiece micrometer, marked with rectangular spaces, I studied and portrayed the subjects. I was able to differentiate the fringes with their lobes and spines. Harry later used these drawings as the basis for distinguishing one type of these insects from another.

The work that Anna and Harry were doing was truly groundbreaking They were discovering things about insects that no one had ever known before, or at least published

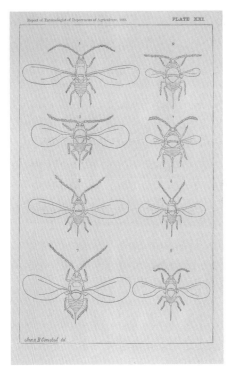

Illustration for <u>Handbook of Nature Study</u>

before. Only one published book could give them any real help in studying the scale bugs. That book was written by a French scientist named Signoret. Harry sent some of his specimens as well as one of Anna's drawings to Mr. Signoret. He wrote back: "The drawing is magnificent. It was made by the hand of a master. I wish I could make as good a one."

Soon after, a colleague spoke to Harry about Anna's drawings in the government report the two had done: "It was the rarest thing that she made a mistake or overlooked anything, and she found lots of things that I did not see in my descriptions."

Until she received this high praise from these noted authorities in the field, Anna looked upon her work as just "good." Modestly, she didn't realize how good. With Mr. Signoret's and the other colleague's encouragement, Anna grew more serious about embarking on a career as a natural history artist.

Anna's interest in becoming a natural history artist shows that career choices can come in different ways to different people. Harry knew from an early age that he wanted to study nature—insects, in particular. Anna, however, probably never gave a thought to drawing sketches of insects until she began doing so for Harry. Even then, she was not preparing for a career. She was merely helping her husband.

Anna, however, may have had a talent for art that she nurtured in an unusual way. For instance, she had always had strong powers of observation. Even as a youngster she captured in her writing details of people, places, and things. Here are some examples from Anna's notes.

Description of Mrs. Allen's home:

Their home was a rambling structure in beautiful grounds at the edge of the village. To me it was a symbol of luxury, elegance, and culture. The mahogany furniture of the parlor and the library, the bookcases filled with books, the handsome silver table service, the spacious sitting room with comfortable chairs and piano, impressed me profoundly.

Description of a classmate:

Julia Thomas, tall and slim, was dressed in a masculine fashion, her skirt reaching to her shoetops, while ours barely cleared the ground. Her short hair and her sailor hat and cape coat added to her appearance of masculinity. She had a strong face and keen eyes. Her charm of manner made her every word interesting.

Description of a lecturer:

He read his lectures from a manuscript with the inflection of a country schoolboy who lets his voice slide down at every period.

As busy as she was, Anna decided to add one more task to her workweek. She decided to resume taking classes and get her degree from Cornell. She had been learning a great deal through her work with Harry. But she felt more training in the sciences would be a big aid in the work she did in entomology.

> OUR OLD FARM AT CORNELL.
>
> When dawn her bowstring drew −
> When her brightest arrows fell −
> They touched the meadows green
> That surround our fair Cornell.
> Hovering rains blew gently o'er,
> Winds their secrets love to tell
> To the grass and bending grain
> On the old farm at Cornell.
>
> The waves below that break
> On Cayuga's fern-clad shore,
> In white caps raise their heads,
> Lifting high to see still more
> Of the land that far above
> On the hill in silence lies,
> Basking in the sun that shines
> Warmly down from pensive skies.
>
> 'Tis land that tells the world
> How to mine the depths below
> And change the buried gold
> Into harvest's ruddy glow.
> Great the power of brain with brawn !
> You have taught the lesson well,
> And your sons will think and work
> Though they're far from you, Cornell.
>
> Oft golden harvest's store
> You have reaped from hill and dell;
> A store of loyal love
> You have reaped from us, Cornell.
> You have given our hearts new warmth
> And our hands new strength can tell −
> While both hearts and hands shall show
> Truest faith in you, Cornell.
>
>   Anna Botsford Comstock.
>
> Tune :− Music in the Air.

The Old Fam at Cornell, by Anna

Anna was also interested in wood engraving. Harry had for years been working on a book called Introduction to Entymology. He was relying on Anna to illustrate it.

Anna thought photographs of wood engravings of insects would enhance the book. In a magazine she saw an advertisement for engraving tools and a set of directions. She sent for them and, as she said, "with my usual daring on untried paths I went at it."

Anna had many qualities that most successful people have. For one thing, she was not content to "rest on her laurels." Even though she was very active and successful, she wanted to finish her studies and graduate. She wanted to strengthen her background in the sciences to enhance her work. And she was not afraid to take a chance. Though she knew very little about wood engraving, she would try to learn. She was not afraid to try.

Wood engraving is not easy, as Anna found out. One of her early teachers described her work as "very curious." Anna wasn't sure what that meant but she didn't think that was praise. In addition, the muscles in her arms began to feel sore, which meant Anna was doing something wrong. But she stayed with it.

At one point she decided to go to New York City to study wood engraving at Cooper Union. Anna described the studio.

> The room assigned to our engraving class was long, high, and rather dingy. It was well lighted by windows on one side, and by an arrangement of sash shades the light came in above our heads and fell upon our work. The opposite wall was hung with well-selected specimens of wood engravings. We sat at one long table; each of us worked on a block of wood, placed upon a leather cushion filled with sand to insure solidity.

Even more impressive to her was her teacher, a Mr. John P. Davis. He was a pleasant man who laughed a lot. When he criticized students' work, he did so in a kind and tactful way. "We felt honored rather than disgraced," Anna said. And he let these art students know that an artist is more than a technician. He conveyed the need to "see and feel and live." He often read poetry aloud as students worked. Sometimes he sang. "Small excuse we had," Anna said, "if we did not become masters."

Some time later, Anna was working on engravings for Harry's entomology book. She sent some samples to her former teacher, Mr. Davis, for his opinion. She was a bit fearful, concerned he might not think the engravings were very good. He sent his evaluation in a note. It read:

> I can hardly believe you trembled when you (sent me) the proofs of your admirable work. To me they are a cause for wonderment and admiration. I notice an earnest study of Marsh (a great engraver) in their technique; and then you have the knowledge of your subject....These little insects seem to possess a superlative accuracy such as no mere engraver could give. Proud as I am to own you as my pupil, I can but feel that in this department of our art you could be my teacher.

When the manuscript for the book finally went to the printer, it contained many of Anna's engravings and illustration. Harry chose a publisher who used a high-quality printer. He wanted to be sure Anna's artwork would be given the best possible showcase. The artwork was so important to the book that Harry referred to it not as "my" book but as "our" book.

These experiences had given Anna confidence in her work. So she sent a number of her drawings to the New Orleans Exposition of 1885. Anna's work won her first honorable mention. Thrilled, she took up her work with new vigor. At her teacher's urging, Anna created an engraving she called "moonlight sonata." Its subject was several night moths. She submitted it to the World's Fair of 1893, held in Chicago. Anna and both her parents traveled to the fair. How pleased they all were to see Anna's work displayed with that of the great masters.

A student at Cornell once again, Anna participated in a number of student activities. Since she was last a student, a new element had been introduced to the women students–the sorority. A sorority is a club or society of women only. Some called it a "sisterhood." Today many colleges have many different sororities.

Anna's engraving of night moths

Anna was not in favor of sororities because she thought they were not democratic. She thought they were secretive and exclusive. Members would accept or reject a woman on personal grounds alone. Anna thought a sorority based on a common interest would be fine. But to reject a woman because "we don't like her" was not Anna's way of doing things.

She went to talk to the college president, Dr. White, about it. He suggested that she join the sorority. He felt she would be a good influence on the other members. So Anna applied and was accepted into the sorority.

Anna's Sigma Xi diploma

She did exert a positive influence. She got the "sisters" in her sorority to broaden their range of interests and activities. She impressed upon them a sense of responsibility that they all had to the university. And she helped to open the channels of communication with other sororities, so theirs was not such an isolated, exclusive club. Dr. White no doubt saw Anna's leadership qualities. And he was correct in thinking she would use those qualities to good advantage in shaping the sorority system at Cornell.

Anna later wrote that she enjoyed the companionship she shared with her sorority sisters. She maintained close contact with some of those women for more than 40 years after graduation.

Besides going to classes, Anna continued to attend lectures. These talks were given on a range of subjects by different experts in their fields. The lectures might be on topics totally unrelated to her studies. Sometimes the speakers would be members of the faculty; sometimes they would be experts from outside the college.

One night Anna attended a lecture that fascinated her. The topic was public institutions-places and organizations operated by the government. Anna began to learn about how these institutions serve the people. As a follow-up to the lecture, Anna visited some of these institutions. She toured a state mental hospital, a county courthouse, a prison, and a reformatory. She saw the whole experience as valuable training for citizenship. This involvement in the way organizations serve the public struck a chord in Anna.

Anna's Cornell Diploma

Not long after that, Anna was asked to give a talk to the Farmer's Institute. This group of farm women met occasionally to learn from one another. Having grown up on a farm, Anna knew the hard life that women on the farm lived. Through the research Harry had done explaining how insects can destroy crops—research that Anna illustrated—she knew full well the difficulties farmers had to endure. Anna didn't speak about the drudgery of a farm life, however. She spoke instead about the happy side of farm life. Her message cheered the women who then went home feeling a bit happier with their lives.

When Anna and Harry next visited her parents' farm, she took time to look at it again, closely.

> We spent our days on my home farm and I renewed my acquaintance with the trees of the virgin forest, still standing near the house, and with the birds—the hermit, wood, and Wilson thrushes, the teacher bird, and many others. The view from the farm was magnificent: rolling hills with their farmsteads, and along the western horizon, blue Lake Erie.

Anna never lost her love for the farm. That love, coupled with her new-found interest in public agencies, would later propel her into her leadership role in the study of nature in schools.

5
Seeing the World

As Harry continued to work on finding a number of useful articles written in German. He thought spending some time in Germany would help him improve his German. So he and Anna set sail for Europe.

Anna was thrilled when they entered an art gallery in Berlin, Germany. She saw exhibited there a group of her own engravings of moths and butterflies. They were displayed in a case right near the entrance. To have traveled so far from home and find her work on display gave her a sense of how highly people valued her work.

Some of what Anna found in Germany displeased her. For one, she thought the government gave people too little freedom and the military too much favor. Anna saw that people walking on a narrow sidewalk would have to step into the street to let a "haughty" officer pass. That "went

Engraving for the <u>Handbook of Nature Study</u>

against the grain," she noted. When one woman refused to step aside for a soldier, he lifted her by the elbows and deposited her in the street.

When visiting the University in Leipzig, Harry met an old friend from the states. He was giving a lecture and invited Harry to attend. Women were not admitted to the university but the professor made special arrangements for Anna to attend the lecture. She had to arrive early and leave late—before and after the regular students. Anna attended, but seemed not too happy with the arrangement.

She thought the German women were too "servile to their lords and masters." The woman in whose home Anna and Harry stayed was a good example. She thought that it improper for Harry to carry items home from a shopping trip. She thought the wife, not the husband, should always carry such bundles.

Anna at the Church of San Pamerazio

Seeing the World

Even back in the United States, Anna found that not every university was as open to women as Cornell was. When she and Harry visited Stanford University in California, Anna was permitted to have only breakfast in the men-only dining room. She had to eat lunch and dinner in her room.

Years later, when Anna and Harry decided to take some time off, they traveled to Egypt, Greece, Italy, Switzerland, and France. Anna, of course, viewed everything with the eye of the artist. At a time when there was no television, and even photographs of people in other countries were rare, first-person written accounts such as the ones Anna wrote were all that most Americans had.

In Egypt she took note of the people, especially the women of different nationalities living there. She also observed the children.

> The *Egyptian* women were clothed in black, and their eyes looked out on the world above their black veils. Over the lower part of their faces, the *Turkish* women wore white veils, some thin enough to show their features. The *Bedouin* women swung along with a second upper black skirt over their heads, their unveiled faces swarthy and purposeful. But of whatever nationality, each woman carried her small child astride one shoulder, one little leg down its mother's back and one on her breast where she could hold it firmly when necessary, and its little arms were clasped around her covered head.
>
> The native boys were amusing, all in nightie-like garments reaching almost to their heels. But they were as full of pranks as any properly breeched (in pants) American boy. They played ball and caught on behind carriages; they wrestled and ran and were full of mischief.

Bridge Over River, watercolor by Anna

Seeing the World

Woman With Donkey, watercolor by Anna

Sundial in Anna's Garden, watercolor by Anna

Seeing the World

Anna's Garden with Sundial and Risley Tower, watercolor by Anna

As Anna's skills matured, she began taking on engraving and illustration assignments for various publications and individuals. This was another way for her to earn money.

Over the years she created her own studio. She often borrowed works from some of the masters in the field and invited visitors to the studio to view them. She enjoyed explaining—through the works on display—the intricacies of engraving. She helped visitors to realize that the way these artists achieved color and texture in wood turned these engravers into artists. Anna felt rewarded to see people appreciating engraving as a true art for the first time.

View of Cayuga Lake, pastel by Anna

Seeing the World

The Lodge –Later home of Anna and Harry

The American Society of Wood Engravers recognized Anna's outstanding contribution to the field by electing her into their membership. She was only the third woman elected to this organization.

Not long after, Anna made another trip to California. This time she brought with her some of her engravings as well as those of the Society. She used these in giving lectures on the subject to various groups. One group included the wife of California's governor. She invited Anna to the governor's mansion for dinner.

People attending Anna's lectures were very impressed. Many even bought some of the works she had with her. In taking this kind of initiative, Anna showed her true pioneer

The Living Room at the Lodge

spirit. She was bringing a totally new art form to a part of the country in which it was rare. In a brief lecture she would try to explain what makes wood engraving more than a craft, but an art. And she did it. She possessed the knowledge, the confidence, the charm, and the speaking ability to do what even long-time members of The American Society of Wood Engravers had not done.

Not all of Anna's California experiences were totally pleasant. Certainly not the one she had in San Francisco. But her spunk won the day for her. After she spoke to the Women's Club of San Francisco, a number of the members asked her to exhibit the engravings to the students at the Art Academy in the city. Anna said she would be happy to.

But when she arrived at the Art Academy, the man in charge said she could not hold the exhibit. He said there was no money budgeted to pay her for the exhibit. She assured the man she did not expect or want to be paid.

Engraved nature card sent to Martha Van Rensselaer

Nature Engraving

She then gave him the names of the women from the Women's Club who had asked her to exhibit at the Academy. The man was not persuaded. He called in

Engraving of Forest Path

another man, who also said there was no money available for the exhibit. Here's what happened next, in Anna's words:

> By that time I was angry and determined to go ahead. I put up the exhibit alone, no one offering to help me; the Grand Mogul (the man in charge) dropped in twice meanwhile, to tell me that there was no money in it for me. I smiled at him, thanked him, and went on hanging the engravings, which was no small job. Then I sat down to await the visitors. Soon they came, at first a few, but on the second day the room was full. That night the Grand Mogul came, apologized for his attitude, and excused it by saying that people were always trying to beat the Academy. I said, 'Well, now you know that there was someone who was glad to do something for the Academy without any compensation, and maybe there will be others.' He thanked me and called the janitor to help take down the pictures. I departed, triumphant.

In 1895, the Comstocks' *Manual for the Study of Insects* was printed. Reviewers gave both its text and its artwork high praise. Within one month, 30 colleges and universities adopted the book for their students. Harry and Anna saw that the book would be reprinted often, so they formed their own publishing company. At first they thought they would have only one book to print and sell—the Manual. But in time, this industrious couple had created a thriving publishing company.

More importantly, the *Manual for the Study of Insects* "fulfilled all and more of our dreams of its usefulness," Anna wrote. "It was the means of bringing knowledge of insects to the general public." That interest in the practical use of this knowledge still drove Anna's work.

Besides serving as a textbook for college students, the *Manual* was used in schools and public libraries. From 1895 to 1926 (when Anna wrote her notes), the book had sold 50,000 copies.

Never comfortable just resting on their laurels, Anna and Harry began work on their next book, *Insect Life*. This book would be very different from the *Manual*. It would be for teachers of young children to use, or as a starting point for a person without knowledge of the subject. The book discussed insect life of the pond, the brook, the orchard, the forest, and the roadside. The book gave directions for collecting insects and studying their life histories. Anna engraved many new illustrations, adding something new— engravings of landscapes.

In addition, *Insect Life* helped nurture the budding nature study movement. And, as you will see, Nature Study would become the focal point of Anna's professional life for the rest of her days.

6

Driving the Nature Study Movement

In the early 1890s, an agricultural depression hit the Eastern part of the United States. New York State was hit especially hard. Farmers were barely making enough money to survive. In fact, many farmers had to sell off their farms and seek jobs elsewhere. Young people, particularly, who might normally work the family farm, were moving away. Because the farm could not generate enough income to support them, these young people headed for work in cities.

The situation became serious enough that officials in New York State knew something had to be done. They called for a meeting of agriculture experts from around the state to look into the problem. The question was posed: "What is the matter with the land in New York State that it cannot support its own population?" Because the State College of Agriculture was set up at Cornell, the University was invited to attend this meeting. Anna attended as the University's representative.

After hours of discussion, the group agreed that one of the main reasons for the depression was "poor farming." That is, farmers were not succeeding in large part because of the methods they were using. They were not cultivating the soil to their best advantage. They were not using the information about nature that was available. For instance, farmers often lost crops because of pests. Mr. Comstock and others had uncovered a great deal of information about pest control. But many of these farmers knew nothing of it.

The committee decided that education would be the key to reviving farming in New York. The group thought the best way to do that was by teaching children in these rural areas about nature. Giving youngsters a fresh look at the soil, the insects and animals, the plants and trees would spur their interest in farming. At the same time it would teach them to find and use the latest information and the best techniques for farming.

The University would play a major role in this nature study effort. And at the forefront of the movement was Anna B. Comstock.

Working with a small group of dedicated individuals, Anna gave many hours to the nature study movement. Anna and her team first examined the state of nature study at the moment. "We don't want to reinvent the wheel," Anna said. "Let's find out what the children are learning about nature in school now. Then we can build on that."

Anna and the others visited a number of schools in rural New York to examine their nature study programs. What they found was "almost no nature study teaching anywhere."

Today that might seem strange. Today children begin studying nature as early as kindergarten, even in pre-school. Almost every American child searches for different kinds of leaves in the fall and brings them to class. They study rocks and birds and insects. But in the 1890s, there was almost no formal study of nature in schools.

So Anna and the others began writing and printing leaflets for teachers. These leaflets gave teachers information they could use in their classrooms to begin bringing nature study to their students.

Next they created the "Junior Naturalist Club." The club had chapters throughout the state. The purpose: to give interested students more opportunity to learn about nature. These clubs quickly caught on and had as many as 30,000 members throughout rural New York.

The clubs often set a specific focus for themselves. For instance, one club focused mainly on birds. The members

Junior Naturalist Club

decided to have a contest. They formed teams to compete against one another. The team that observed the highest number of different types of bird would win. How could the judges tell if a team had actually observed a bird close up? The members took careful notes on each bird. At the end of the time period, each team submitted its notes.

Anna was pleased with the overwhelming response to the idea of nature clubs. "It's another good sign," she said, "that youngsters want to know more about nature.

Anna asked to meet with members of the State Department of Education in Albany, the New York State capital. Anna decided she would give a little "push" to the state officials, to get them moving. They, in turn, would "push" the schools.

In addition, Anna traveled throughout the state giving talks to various teachers' groups and institutes. She helped them see how serious the farming situation was. She encouraged them to see that a real solution was available. And she explained that they—the teachers—were the ones to deliver that solution.

She also traveled out of state, as other states were interested in learning about the nature study movement taking place in New York. On a trip to Grand Rapids, Michigan, Anna was a speaker on the same program as the famous Booker T. Washington.

Anna scheduled summer sessions at Cornell, for teachers to come and learn more about nature study. She didn't know if anyone would come but she prepared a rigorous three-week program. "What if no one shows up?" she asked.

She was shocked—pleasantly—when 100 classroom teachers showed up for the first session. These teachers—to be students for the three weeks—spent two days each week learning about insect life. They spent two days studying plants. And the fifth day of each week was given to "general agricultural studies."

Besides organizing the program, Anna did much of the teaching. One of the classes she taught was in "farm library." She wanted to give these teachers—and eventually their students—a love of books on nature and natural history. She included poetry readings about nature. Ever the scientist, Anna was always the well-rounded educator. She never lost sight of the human element behind the scientific research.

Besides teaching teachers, Anna also spoke to groups of students. She once was asked to speak to the seventh and eight graders at the school in Perry, New York. When Anna arrived at the school she found not only 300 students from the upper grades but also 200 students from the primary grades.

> I was at my wit's end, for it is very difficult to hold the interest of small wrigglers while talking to older pupils. I had an inspiration. I began by saying that I had a pet at home. Guess what it is. Many guesses were made, none of them right. My pet was a scarlet oak tree and I told how its leaves had to prepare its own food, how it lived and breathed and blossomed, and how its acorns scattered. Guess how old my pet tree is? Many guesses—all wrong. It is 400 years old; and then I told them of all my pet tree had seen over those 400 years—Indians, panthers, bears, wolves, deer.

Through her leadership and teaching, her books and other publications, and through her dedication, Anna drove the spread of nature study. Not only were teachers in rural New York counties teaching nature studies. But so were teachers in the cities and in schools in states all across the country. In addition, nature study was now a recognized academic course in many colleges and universities.

For the second summer session for teachers, Anna received another surprise. Most of the teachers who enrolled came from city schools. The program was designed for teachers in rural schools, so their students would stay on the farms and succeed. But the teachers from city schools wanted their children to learn about nature too. What was Anna to do?

She settled the issue in three ways. First, she arranged to have the summer sessions in the local areas where the rural teachers taught and lived. In that way, these teachers would be sure to get a "place" in the classes. Second, Anna and her team decided to publish more material on nature study. In that way teachers everywhere could use it. And third, Anna went into the cities to try to build a nature study program around the produce sold in city markets. She ran an experiment at the Allen Street School in New York City to launch the study of nature from market produce.

As busy as she was, Anna never passed up an opportunity to help people learn if they wanted to. By 1903, Anna had written enough pamphlets and articles to fill a book. So her

Anna reading in the garden

writings were collected and published in *Ways of the Six-Footed*. Though she had worked on a number of Harry's books, this was the first book for which Anna did all of the writing and illustrating.

Anna continued to give lectures and seminars on nature study throughout the country. She spoke at Columbia Teachers College in New York City; the University of Virginia in Charlottesville, Virginia; and the University of California, Hillcrest campus. Whenever possible, Anna included literature of nature in her talks.

She continued to conduct the summer sessions in Nature Study for teachers. These sessions were now held in Chautauqua, New York. At one of these sessions she found that many of the teachers had little or no background in science. So Anna tried to get each person in the class interested in some phase of nature that she could follow by herself. Anna used trees, ferns, birds, and butterflies for these "individualized" programs.

Anna's reputation was spreading. Publishers were approaching her to write books for them to publish. With Harry she wrote *How to Know Butterflies*. When a publisher asked her to write a book on bees, Anna wrote *How to Keep Bees*.

But these books would be only warm-ups for what was to come next.

7

Anna's Handbook of Nature Study

People across the country, especially teachers, were looking for more and more direction for teaching nature study. Nature study was important not only for children in farm areas. Teachers realized that all children needed to learn about the world they live in. Education offered the best way to protect the earth, and sea, and sky, and all their creatures.

The clamoring for more materials, information, and direction, put an idea in Anna's head. "Why not write a handbook on nature study for teachers?" Many teachers flocked to the classes and lectures Anna gave. But many others could not get to these sessions. Yet they too wanted to teach their students about nature.

Harry looked at the project from the standpoint of a publisher. "I really don't think a book like that will sell," he said. "Aside from the time you will spend writing and illustrating it, you will probably lose about $5000.00 in printing costs. But if you want to do it," he added, "I'll be happy to help in any way I can."

Anna appreciated Harry's honest opinion and his willingness to help even on a project he thought would fail. That says a great deal about how much he loved Anna and respected her commitment to her work.

Drawing on her background, her experience working with teachers, and the many leaflets she wrote, Anna began work on *Handbook of Nature Study*. Harry was right about the amount of time Anna would devote to the book. But he was wrong about its popularity.

It first appeared in print in 1911. Teachers quickly bought up all copies in the first printing. And the second. And the third. The *Handbook* was reprinted many times over the years. It is still in print and use today—more than 90 years later. More than 100,000 copies have been sold. It has been translated in eight different languages. That's a "tribute to the durable charm and correctness of the original text," one commentator wrote. He called it Anna's "love affair with nature."

In the Foreword to the 1986 edition, Verne Rockcastle, a noted scholar in the field, said Anna's "*Handbook* has

Harry (John) and Anna

been the natural history bible for countless teachers."

What makes the *Handbook* so effective? For one thing, Anna advises teachers to "make each lesson an investigation and make the students feel they are investigators." That is: don't just tell them things or have them read about nature. Let them go out and study it the way a true scientist does. And like an investigator, let them follow the clues to reach their own conclusions.

In addition, Anna's descriptions are careful and

accurate, but not technical. She uses language that teachers and students can understand. For example, here's her description of the Isabella Tiger Moth, sometimes called the Wooly Bear:

> When we see the Wooly Bear hurrying along in the fall, it is hunting for some cozy place in which to pass the winter. It makes its cocoon, usually in early spring, of silk woven with its own hair. In late spring, it comes forth a yellowish moth with black dots on its wings. (p. 312)

Anna encourages teachers to venture onto what may be new ground for them. "You don't have to be scientists," she says, "or know much about nature" to use the *Handbook* in guiding students in nature study. All you need are an inquiring mind and the ability to observe—by seeing, hearing, smelling, touching, and sometimes tasting.

Anna's approach in the *Handbook* is the same she and Harry used for years in their study of nature. That is, to study each organism—whether insect, bird, flower, butterfly—in its own environment. Examine the organism's features. Find out how those features enable the organism to do what it does. For example:

> When any creature has unusually strong hind legs, we may be sure it is a jumper, and the grasshopper shows this peculiarity at first glance. The front legs are short, the middle legs a trifle longer, but the femur of the hind leg is nearly as long as the entire body. This part of the leg contains many muscles that have the appearance of being braided because of the way they are attached to the skeleton of the leg. The tibia of the hind leg is long and as stiff as if made of steel. (p. 339)

Later in the lesson Anna, relates how the grasshopper uses those legs:

> The grasshopper is especially fitted for living in grassy fields. Its color protects it from being seen by its enemies, the birds. If attacked, it escapes by long jumps and by flight. (p. 341)

Anna's *Handbook* also makes nature study an aesthetic or artistic experience. That is, it opens a person's eyes and mind to the individuality and personality of each of nature's creatures. Anna hoped that studying nature would enrich people's lives. She hoped to help students see the relationship between themselves and the natural world. She cautions teachers: "In the early years we are not to teach nature as a science; we are not to teach it primarily for method or drill; we are to teach it for living."

Anna's approach is easy for teachers to follow. Each lesson begins with the "Teacher's Story." The teacher can learn about the animal or insect or flower before introducing it to students.

Next comes the "Observation Outline." This is a list of questions for students to use in examining the subject on their own. For example, here are a few questions for students that can guide their observation of the Wooly Bear:

> How can you tell the Wooly Bear from all other caterpillars? Are they all colored alike? How many segments of the body are black at the front end? How many are red? Can you see the fleshy legs along the sides of the body? How many legs are there?

Drawing of a caterpillar

Observing the caterpillar up close and answering these questions, students learn first-hand about the caterpillar. They are not given the details in a text. They don't have lists of facts to memorize. Instead, they learn about the caterpillar as Harry and Anna did—by observing it closely.

In some lessons there is a third feature—a poem. The poem shows how the bird or insect or flower being studied has moved one person (the poet). For example, here's a short poem about the flight of the butterfly, included in the lesson on the Wooly Bear:

> Before your sight,
>
> Mounts on the breeze the butterfly, and soars,
>
> Small creature as she is, from earth's bright flowers
>
> Into the dewy clouds.
>
> ~ William Wordsworth

One reason the *Handbook* has been so popular is that it can be used in both the classroom and in the field. That is, students can go into the woods or a garden to examine a subject. Or they can do the same with specimens or illustrations brought into the classroom.

In the *Handbook* Anna gives teachers directions on helping students create their own field notebooks. "These should have a pencil attached and be small enough to fit in a pocket." Students then can have the notebooks handy when they observe creatures. They can quickly and easily take notes of what they see. They can even use these notebooks for taking notes about their own pets.

Pictures and illustrations, of course, appear on almost every page in the *Handbook*. Some of the activities for students involve drawing what they see in nature. Drawing had much to do with Anna's love for nature. So it is expected that she would have students draw as well.

The study of nature, of course, has developed extensively since Anna's time. Even very young students often have the benefit of microscopes and other tools for examining specimens. There are filmstrips and videos. High magnification cameras take us into the tiniest

Anna at the time The Handbook was published

crevices to see how even the tiniest creatures function. But all of what we have today started back in the late 1890s. And one person who played a leading role in making it all happen was Anna B. Comstock—truly a pioneer.

For her work, Anna was named Assistant Professor of Nature Study in the Cornell University Extension Division.

This was the first time a woman held the title of "Professor" at Cornell. But a number of the university's trustees objected to a woman's holding the title "Professor." So the college president had to rescind the title. He changed Anna's title to "Lecturer." Anna, of course, had felt the sting of this kind of gender prejudice before. But that did not soften the pain of this insult. Her feelings were soothed somewhat when the president saw to it that she received the same salary as lecturer that she had received as assistant professor.

Though some prejudices die hard, they do die. Years later, when she was close to retirement, Anna was named full professor at Cornell. That is the highest rank for a teaching faculty member at a college. Anna saw that not only as a tribute to her long service; but she also saw it as a tribute to the Department of Nature Study that she helped develop. She accepted the promotion graciously. She said she was glad her successor would be able to receive the rank of professor, in carrying on the nature study work.

Years later, after she had retired from teaching and had reduced the amount of writing, she had a most pleasant surprise. One day while reading *The New York Times*.

She came across an article on the 12 greatest women in America. The League of Women Voters, a national women's organization, had selected 12 women who had helped and influenced the most number of people. Among the list was Anna B. Comstock. Anna thought it a coincidence that another woman should have the identical name she had. Harry said, "No, Anna. It's you."

"It must be some mistake," Anna said. But no, it was not a mistake. Anna had indeed been included among this most select and prestigious group of women.

Many years later, in 1988, Anna was named to the Conservationist Hall of Fame. She, of course, had died many years before. But she no doubt would have been happy to have her work recognized in this way.

As exciting as those honors would have been, Anna may have been more moved by a gift she received from one of her students—Mary C. Lowe. On Anna's 65th birthday, Mary wrote a short poem. No doubt, that poem spoke for the thousands of students Anna had touched in her lifetime. The poem gets to the heart of what she devoted her life to—enabling people to understand the natural world in which they live.

To Anna B. Comstock

On her sixty-fifth birthday

You show us beauty everywhere,
In flower and bird and tree;
You open windows which look far
Into Infinity.
And we who love these things turn back
Today with word of praise
And grateful hearts to wish you joy
For all the onward ways.
And through the greetings, like a bird,
A something sings and sings
A blessing on you every day,
Interpreter of Things.

Anna B. Comstock

Handbook Lessons for You to Try

You have read about how Anna influenced the growth of nature study. Now you may want to try a few of her lessons for yourself. On the following pages you will find two lessons—one on the housefly and one on goldfish. Go through the lessons just as if you were a student in one of Anna's classes. Follow her instructions for observing and answering. See how the method Anna devised almost 100 years ago is still effective to teach about nature today.

(These lessons are taken from: *Handbook of Nature Study*, by Anna Botsford Comstock. Comstock Publishing Associates, A Division of Cornell University Press, 1986.)

Lesson 87
The Housefly

Leading Thought. The housefly has conquered the world and is found practically everywhere. It breeds in filth and especially in horse manure. It is very prolific; the few flies that manage to pass the winter in this northern climate are the ancestors of the millions which attack us and our food later in the season. These are a menace because they carry germs of disease from sputa and excrement to our tables, leaving them upon our food.

Method. Give out the questions for observation and let the pupils answer them either orally or in their notebooks. If possible, every pupil should look at a housefly through a lens or microscope. If this is not possible, pictures should be shown to demonstrate its appearance.

Observations.

1. Look at a fly, using a lens if you have one. Describe its eyes. Do you see that they have a honeycomb arrangement of little eyes? Can you see, on top of the head between the big eyes, a dot? A microscope reveals this dot to be made of three tiny eyes, huddled together. After seeing a fly's eyes, do you wonder that you have so much difficulty in hitting it or catching it?

2. Can you see the fly's antennae? Do you think that it has a keen sense of smell? Why?

3. How many wings has the fly? How does it differ from the bee in this respect? Can you see two little white objects, one just behind the base of each wing? These are called poisers, or balancers, and all flies have them in some form. 'What is the color of the wings? Are they transparent? Can you see the veins in them? On what part of the body do the wings grow?

4. Look at the fly from below. How many legs has it? From what part of the body do the legs come? 'What is that part of the insect's body called to

which the legs and wings are attached?

5. How does the fly's abdomen look? What is its color and its covering?

6. Look at the fly's legs. How many segments can you see in a leg? Can you see that the segment on which the fly walks has several joints? Does it walk on all of these segments or on the one at the tip?

7. When the fly eats, can you see its tongue? Can you feel its tongue when it rasps your hand? Where does it keep its tongue usually?

8. Describe how a fly makes its toilet as follows: How does it clean its front feet? Its head? Its middle feet? Its hind feet? Its wings?

9. Do you know how flies carry disease? Did you ever see them making their toilet on your food at the table? Do you know what diseases are carried by flies? What must you do to prevent flies from bringing disease to your family?

10. Do you think that a small fly ever grows to be a large fly? How do the young of all kinds of flies look? Do you know where the housefly lays its eggs? On what do the maggots feed? How long before they change to pupae? How long does it take them to grow from eggs to flies? How do the houseflies in our northern climate pass the winter?

11. **Lesson in Arithmetic** — It requires perhaps twenty days to span the time from the eggs of one

generation of the housefly to the eggs of the next, and thus there might easily be five generations in one summer. Supposing the fly which wintered behind the window curtain in your home last winter, flew out to the stables about May 1 and laid 120 eggs in the sweepings from the horse stable, all of which hatched and matured. Supposing one-half of these were mother flies and each of them, in turn, laid 120 eggs, and so on for five generations, all eggs laid developing into flies, and one-half of the flies of each generation being mother flies. How many flies would the fly that wintered behind your curtain have produced by September?

12. Pour some gelatin, unsweetened, on a clean plate. Let a housefly walk around on the gelatin as soon as it is cool; cover the plate to keep out the dust and leave it for two or three days. Examine it then and see if you can tell where the fly walked. What did it leave in its tracks?

13. Write an essay on the housefly, its dangers and how to combat it, basing the essay on bulletins of the United States Department of Agriculture.

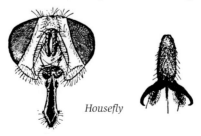

Housefly

Lesson 36
A Study of the Fish

Leading Thought. A fish lives in the water where it must breathe, move, and find its food. The water world is quite different from the air world and the fish have developed forms, senses, and habits which fit them for life in the water.

Method. The goldfish is used as a subject for this lesson because it is so conveniently kept where the children may see it. However, a shiner or other minnow would do as well.

Before the pupils begin the study, place the diagram shown on p. 145 on the black board, with all the parts labeled (diagram follows the questions). Thus the pupils will be able to learn the parts of the fish by consulting it, and not be compelled to commit them to memory arbitrarily. It would be well to associate the goldfish with a geography lesson on China.

Observations.
1. Where do fish live?
2. What is the shape of a fish when seen from above? Where is the widest part? What is its shape seen from the side? Think if you can in how many ways the shape of the fish is adapted for moving swiftly through the water.

3. How many fins has the fish? Make a sketch of the goldfish with all its fins and name them from the diagram on the blackboard. (Diagram follows the questions.)
4. How many fins are there in all? Four of these fins are in pairs; where are they situated? What are they called? Which pair corresponds to our arms? Which to our legs?
5. Describe the pectoral fins. How are they used? Are they kept constantly moving? Do they move together or alternately? How are they used when the fish swims backward?
6. How are the ventral fins used? How do they assist the fish when swimming?
7. Observe a dorsal fin and an anal fin. How are these used when the fish is swimming?
8. With what fin does the fish push itself through the water? Make a sketch of the tail. Note if it is square, rounded, or notched at the end.
9. Watch the goldfish swim and describe the action of all the fins while it is in motion. In what position are the fins when the fish is at rest?
10. What is the nature of the covering of the fish? Are the scales large or small? In what direction do they seem to over lap? Of what use to the fish is this scaly covering?

Handbook Lessons for You to Try

11. Can you see a line which extends from the upper part of the gill opening, along the side to the tail? This is called the lateral line. Do you think it is of any use to the fish?

12. Note carefully the eyes of the fish. Describe the pupil and the iris. Are the eyes placed so that the fish can see in all directions? Can they be moved so as to see better in any direction? Does the fish wink? Has it any eyelids? Do you know why fish are nearsighted?

13. Can you see the nostrils? Is there a little wartlike projection connected with the nostril? Do you think fishes breathe through their nostrils?

14. Describe the mouth of the fish. Does it open upward, downward, or directly in front? What sort of teeth have fish? How does the fish catch its prey? Does the lower or upper jaw move in the process of eating?

15. Is the mouth kept always in motion? Do you think the fish is swallowing water all the time? Do you know why it does this? Can you see a wide opening along the sides of the head behind the gill cover? Does the gill cover move with the movement of the mouth? How does a fish breathe?

16. What are the colors of the goldfish above and below? What would happen to our beautiful goldfish if they were put in a brook with other

fish? Why could they not hide? Do you know what happens to the colors of the goldfish when they run wild in our streams and ponds?

17. Can you find in books or cyclopedias where the goldfish came from? Are they gold and silver in color in the streams where they are native? Do you think that they had originally the long, slender, swallow-tails which we see sometimes in gold fish? How have the beautiful colors and graceful forms of the gold and silver fishes been developed?

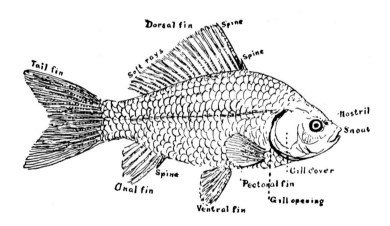

Goldfish

The Oracle of the Goldfishes

By James Russell Lowell

I have my world, and so have you,
    A tiny universe for two,
    A bubble by the artist blown,
Scarcely more fragile than our own,
Where you have all a whale could wish,
    Happy as Eden's primal fish.
    Manna is dropt you thrice a day
From some kind heaven not far away,
And still you snatch its softening crumbs,
Nor, more than we, think whence it comes.
    No toil seems yours but to explore
Your cloistered realm from shore to shore;
Sometimes you trace its limits round,
Sometimes its limpid depths you sound,
    Or hover motionless midway,
    Like gold-red clouds at set of day;
Erelong you whirl with sudden whim
Off to your globe's most distant rim,
Where, greatened by the watery lens,
    Methinks no dragon of the fens
    Flashed huger scales against the sky,
    Roused by Sir Bevis or Sir Guy;
And the one eye that meets my view,
Lidless and strangely largening, too,

Like that of conscience in the dark,
Seems to make me its single mark.
What a benignant lot is yours
That have an own All-out-of-doors,
No words to spell, no sums to do,
No Nepos and no parlyvoo!
How happy you, without a thought
Of such cross things as Must and Ought—
I too the happiest of boys
To see and share your golden joys!

List of Anna's Publications
Books That Anna Wrote
1903 *Ways of the Six-Footed*. Illustrated.
1904 *How to Know the Butterflies*. With Harry. Illustrated.
1905 *How to Keep the Bees*. Illustrated.
1906 *Confessions of a Heathen*. Fictional novel.
1911 *Handbook of Nature Study*. Illustrated.
1914 *The Pet Book*.
1915 *Trees at Leisure*.
1920 *Nature Notebook Series*.

Books That Harry Wrote on Which Anna Worked
1888 *An Introduction to Entymology*. Illustrations and engravings by Anna.
1895 *A Manual for the Study of Insects*. Illustrations by Anna.
1896 *Insect Life*. Writing and illustrations by Anna.

About the author...

Cos Ferrara has been a writer for 25 years. A former teacher, he has written for students as well as adults. He brings to the Girls Explore books his experience as a father of three and grandfather of five. His message to our readers is: "The world is large and full of wonder and opportunity. Go out and explore it."